I0816243

ANIMAL ALBUMS
THE
SNAKE
FAMILY
BY GOLRIZ GOLKAR
eureka!
EUREKA!, AN IMPRINT OF BELLWETHER MEDIA BY FLUTTERBEE

Eureka! books turn real stories into unforgettable experiences. Clear, direct language and sharp, captivating imagery make it easy to follow your curiosity, one fascinating fact at a time.
Your Eureka! moment awaits!

This edition first published in 2026 by Bellwether Media, Inc.

Text copyright © 2026 by Bellwether Media, Inc. All rights reserved. No part of this publication may be reproduced, stored in any retrieval system, or transmitted in any form or by any means, electronic, mechanical, photocopying, recording, or otherwise, without written permission of the publisher.

EUREKA! and associated logos are trademarks and/or registered trademarks of Bellwether Media, Inc. Bellwether Media is a division of FlutterBee Education Group.

For information regarding permission, write to Bellwether Media, Inc., Attention: Permissions Department, 3500 American Blvd W, Suite 150, Bloomington, MN 55431.

Library of Congress Cataloging-in-Publication Data is available at www.loc.gov or upon request from the publisher.

ISBN: 9798893048582 (hardcover)
ISBN: 9798893049589 (ebook)

Editor: Rebecca Sabelko   Designer: Josh Brink   Series Designer: Jeff Kollock

Printed in the United States of America, North Mankato, MN.

TABLE OF CONTENTS

WHAT ARE SNAKES?

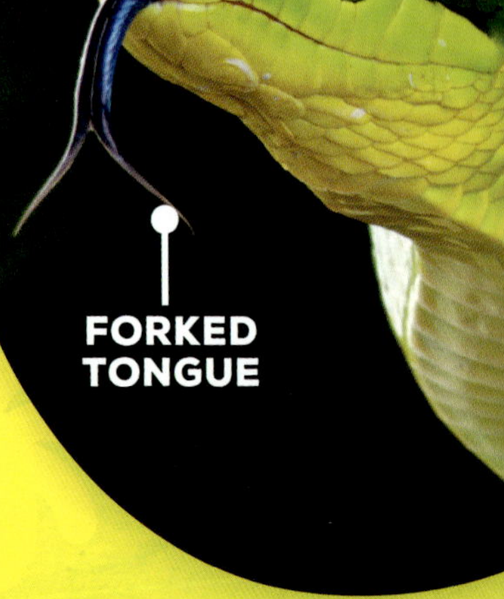

Snakes are reptiles in the *Serpentes* suborder. There are more than 3,000 snake species in the world. They live on every continent except Antarctica. These animals live in a wide range of habitats. They can be found in deserts, grasslands, forests, and oceans.

BUSH VIPER

Snakes are diverse. But they share some features and behaviors. All snakes are cold-blooded. They shed their skin. Snakes have forked tongues that they use to collect scents in the air or water around them. As meat eaters, these animals play important roles in keeping food chains healthy around the world.

SHEDDING SKIN

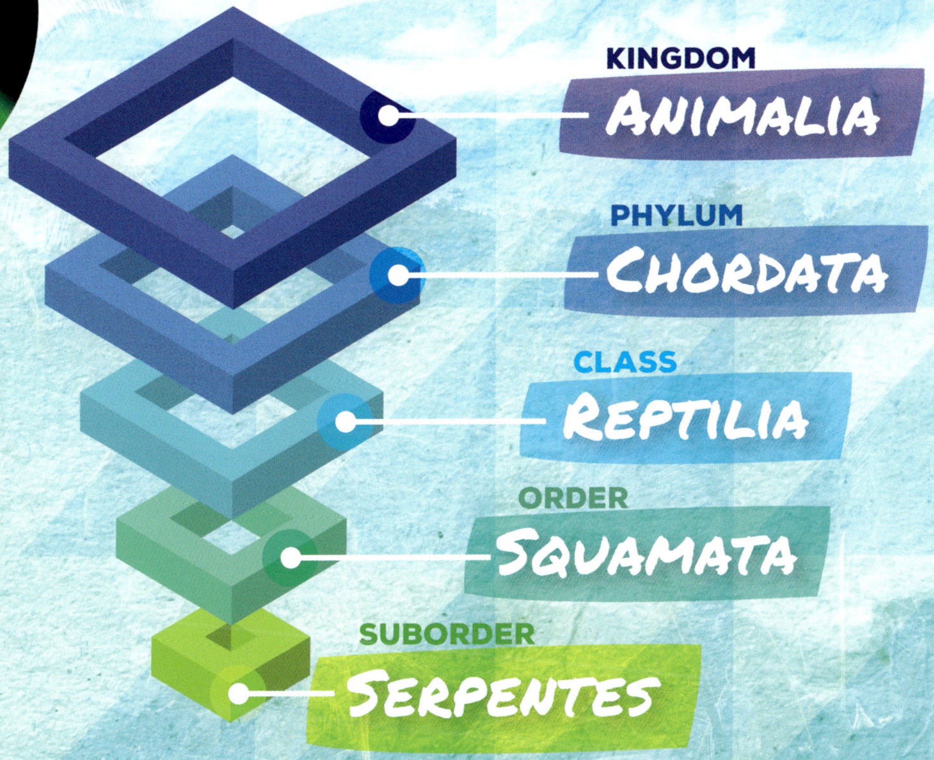

KINGDOM
ANIMALIA

PHYLUM
CHORDATA

CLASS
REPTILIA

ORDER
SQUAMATA

SUBORDER
SERPENTES

TAXONOMY CHART

BANDED SEA SNAKE ▲

▲
GREAT LAKES BUSH VIPER

THE HISTORY OF SNAKES

Snakes began to evolve from lizards more than 100 million years ago. Early snakes likely spent a lot of time underground. Their bodies adapted to tight spaces. They became longer. Their legs got shorter and eventually disappeared. In time, their long, legless bodies helped them easily climb trees and move across land and water.

OLIVE SEA SNAKE

EMERALD TREE BOA

Earth's thousands of snake species have many adaptations to help them thrive. Snakes adapted flexible jaws to eat many types of prey. They developed forked tongues and organs that sense chemicals to find prey. They evolved methods of defense and hunting such as using venom or constriction.

EVOLUTIONARY EXCELLENCE

LIFE CYCLE

Baby snakes are called snakelets. They are born in different ways. Around 70 percent of snake species lay eggs. Other species give birth to live snakelets that never developed in eggs. There are also species in which snakelets grow in eggs inside their mothers' bodies. After they hatch, their mothers give birth.

SNAKE EGG

GARTER SNAKE WITH SNAKELETS

CORN SNAKE HATCHING

Snakelets look like small adults. Most can live on their own right after birth. Mothers may give birth to over 100 snakelets at a time. Some snakes have young once or twice per year. Others reproduce every three years.

AVERAGE LITTER SIZE

WESTERN DIAMONDBACK RATTLESNAKE

12 LIVE SNAKELETS

GREEN ANACONDA

30 LIVE SNAKELETS

YELLOW-BELLIED SEA SNAKE

4 LIVE SNAKELETS

KING COBRA

30 EGGS

SNAKE LANGUAGE AND BEHAVIOR

COMMUNICATION

Nearly all species of snakes live alone. But they seek out others to mate. Females release pheromones to attract males. Males may perform different movements to begin mating.

RATTLESNAKE WARNING

Snakes often use sounds and body language to warn enemies to stay away. Some species hiss or lift their bodies to look bigger. Rattlesnakes shake their rattles as warnings.

BASKING

BEHAVIORS

Snakes must bask to maintain their body temperatures. Those that live in colder climates carry out brumation in winter.

AMAZON TREE BOA MOLTING

SNAKE SKIN

Snakes must shed their skin as they grow. This process is called molting. Molting also removes harmful parasites.

BROWN FOREST COBRA
showing warning behavior

SNAKE FAMILY TREE

PYTHONS

AROUND 40 SPECIES

Female pythons coil their bodies around their eggs to keep them warm. They create more heat by shivering.

BOAS

AROUND 40 SPECIES

Boas are constrictors. These snakes finish prey by cutting off its blood supply.

BURMESE PYTHONS ▲

GREEN ANACONDAS ▲

BOA CONSTRICTORS ▲

VIPERS

MORE THAN 200 SPECIES

Vipers do not always release venom when they bite. They may choose not to because it could take around 14 days to produce more.

▲ WESTERN DIAMONDBACK RATTLESNAKES

▲ EASTERN COPPERHEADS

▲ SIDEWINDERS

SERPENTES

ELAPIDS

AROUND 300 SPECIES

▲KING COBRAS

▲YELLOW-BELLIED SEA SNAKES

▲BLACK MAMBAS

COLUBRIDS

MORE THAN 1,700 SPECIES

▲COMMON GARTER SNAKES

▲SCARLET KINGSNAKES

▲MANGROVE SNAKES

CORN SNAKES ▶

AROUND ▼ **25** OTHER SNAKE FAMILIES

BURMESE PYTHONS

Burmese pythons are some of the largest snakes on Earth.

WHERE DO THEY LIVE?

Burmese pythons are native to Southeast Asia. They are found in rainforests, swamps, grasslands, rocky mountain bases, and river valleys. They go into brumation in tree hollows and burrows.

DIET

Burmese pythons are top predators that mostly eat small mammals and birds. They stalk prey before grabbing it with their sharp teeth. They squeeze prey with their bodies until it stops breathing.

SIZE COMPARISON

23FT (7 m)

Burmese python

3FT (0.9 m)

eastern copperhead

6FT (1.8 m)

corn snake

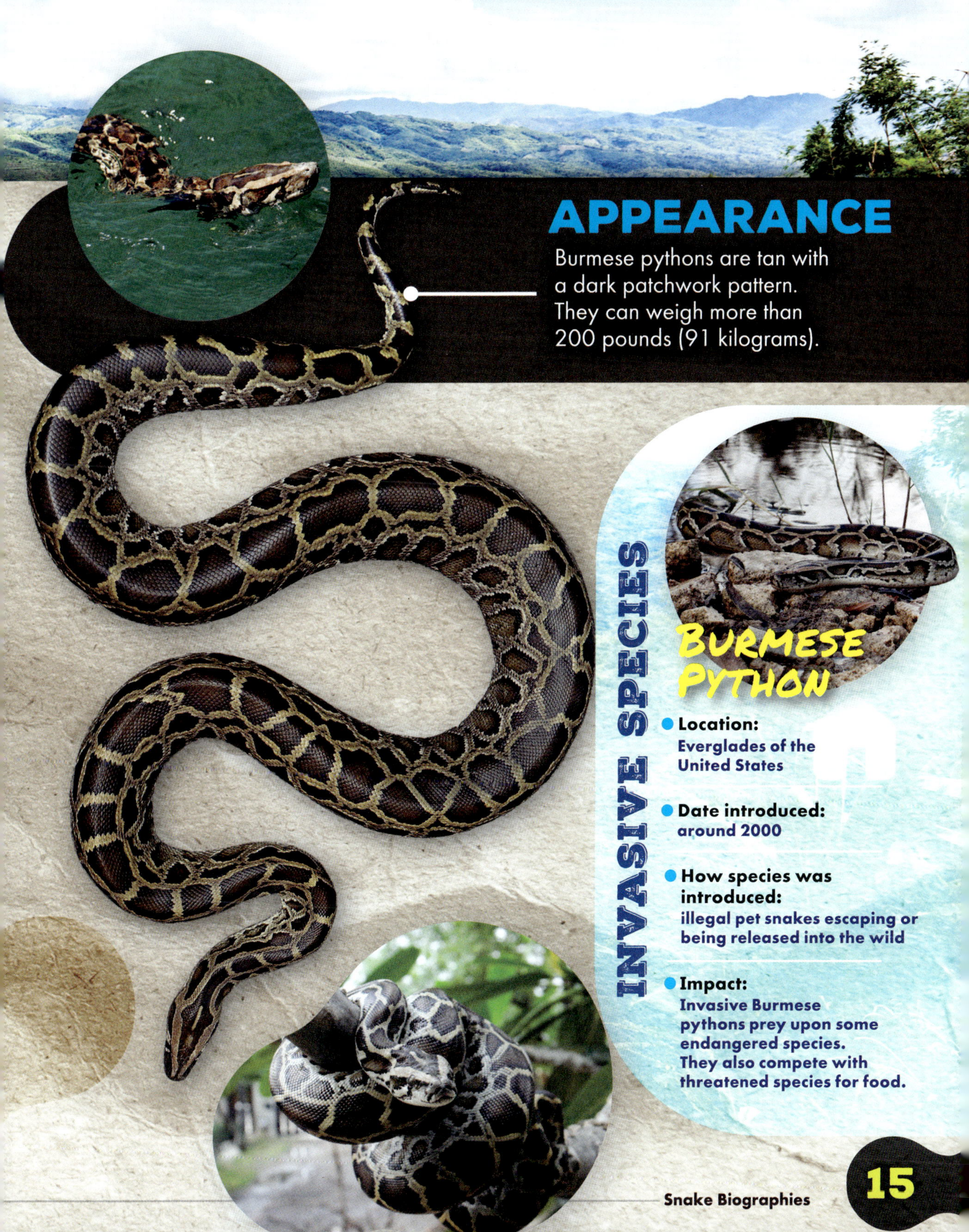

APPEARANCE

Burmese pythons are tan with a dark patchwork pattern. They can weigh more than 200 pounds (91 kilograms).

INVASIVE SPECIES

BURMESE PYTHON

- **Location:** Everglades of the United States
- **Date introduced:** around 2000
- **How species was introduced:** illegal pet snakes escaping or being released into the wild
- **Impact:** Invasive Burmese pythons prey upon some endangered species. They also compete with threatened species for food.

GREEN ANACONDAS

Green anacondas are the heaviest snakes in the world. They can weigh up to 550 pounds (249.5 kilograms).

APPEARANCE

These giant snakes are often olive green with dark, rounded spots across their backs. Dark spots with yellow centers run along their sides.

SIZE COMPARISON

30FT (9.1 m)

green anaconda

23FT (7 m)

Burmese python

3.6FT (1.1 m)

yellow-bellied sea snake

DIET

Green anacondas are top predators. They eat reptiles, birds, and large mammals. They wait underwater to ambush prey. They grab the animal with their powerful jaws. Then they coil their bodies around the animal.

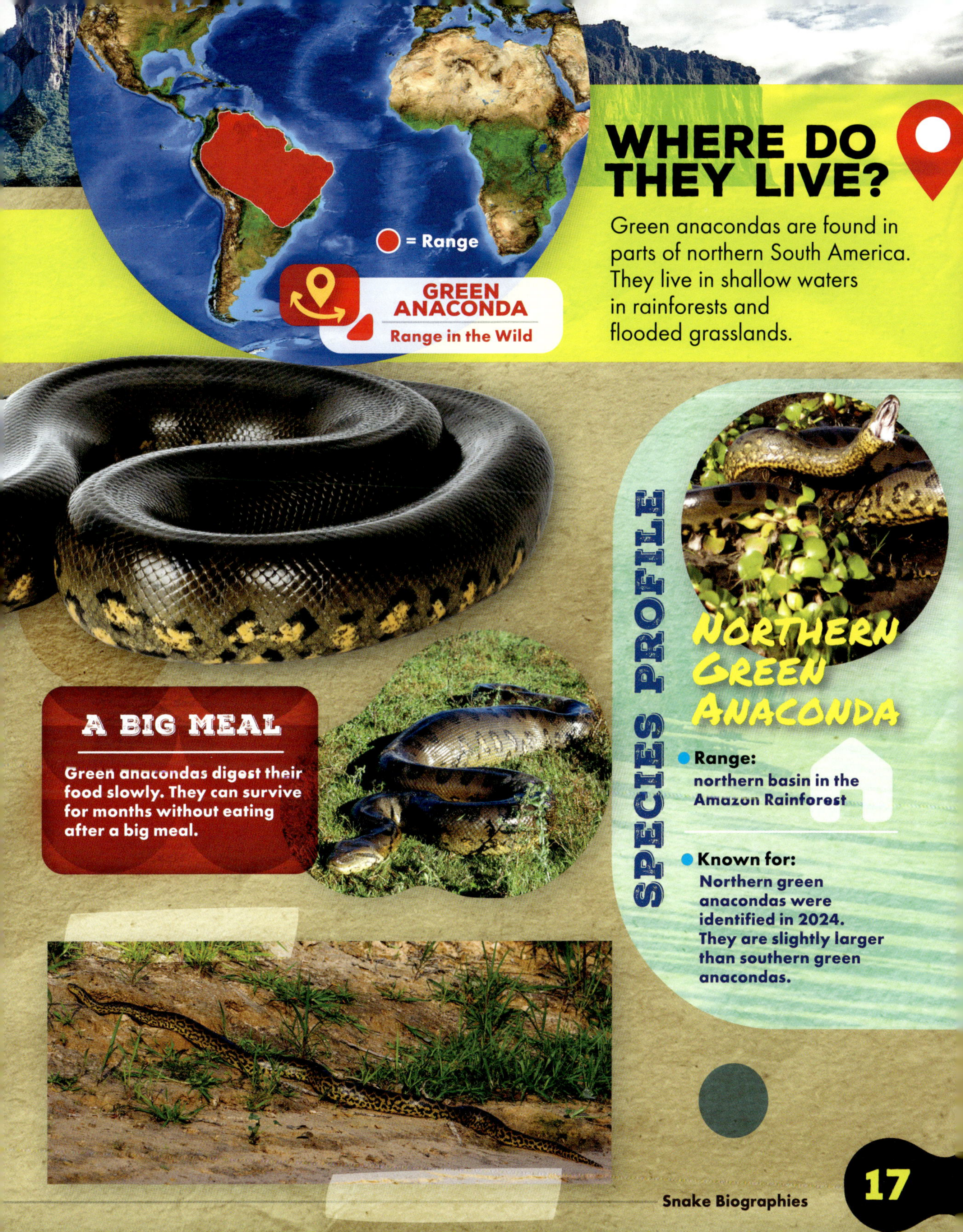

WHERE DO THEY LIVE?

Green anacondas are found in parts of northern South America. They live in shallow waters in rainforests and flooded grasslands.

A BIG MEAL

Green anacondas digest their food slowly. They can survive for months without eating after a big meal.

SPECIES PROFILE

NORTHERN GREEN ANACONDA

- **Range:** northern basin in the Amazon Rainforest
- **Known for:** Northern green anacondas were identified in 2024. They are slightly larger than southern green anacondas.

BOA CONSTRICTORS

There are several subspecies of boa constrictors. Red-tailed boas are the most well-known.

APPEARANCE

Boa constrictors often have a tan pattern of ovals or circles separated by dark spots. Their tails are usually red or brown.

RED-TAILED BOA

◀ MEXICAN WEST COAST BOA

SIZE COMPARISON

13FT (4 m)

boa constrictor

3FT (0.9 m)

eastern copperhead

1.7FT (0.5 m)

scarlet kingsnake

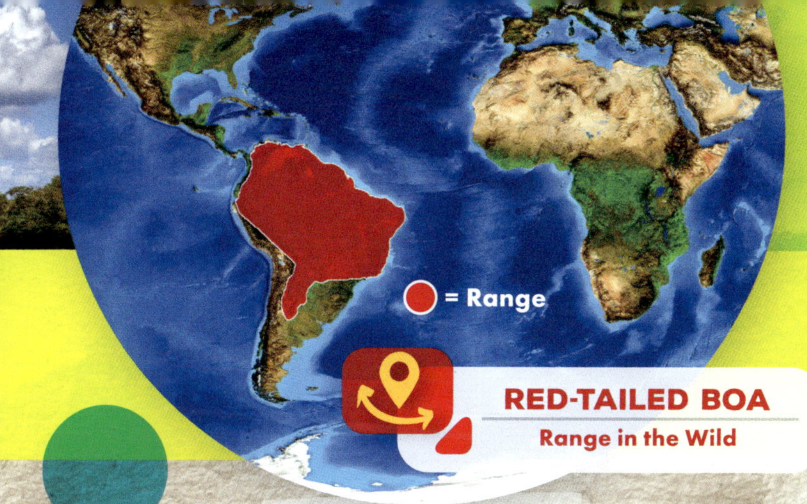

WHERE DO THEY LIVE?

Boa constrictors are native to areas of Mexico, Central America, and South America. They mostly live in the Amazon Rainforest. They are often spotted in water.

SPECIES PROFILE

CENTRAL AMERICAN BOA

- **Range:** parts of Mexico, much of Central America, and areas of northern and central South America
- **Known for:** Central American boas are a common snake in the pet trade. They are often bred to have many different colors and patterns on their backs.

DIET

These snakes use sharp vision, smell, and heat sensors to ambush prey at night. They strike with their pointed, curved teeth. Then they coil around their prey and squeeze it.

WESTERN DIAMONDBACK RATTLESNAKES

Western diamondback rattlesnakes are aggressive vipers. They warn enemies by rattling their tails.

SIZE COMPARISON

5FT (1.5 m)
western diamondback rattlesnake

2.8FT (0.9m)
common garter snake

3.6FT (1.1 m)
yellow-bellied sea snake

WHERE DO THEY LIVE?

These snakes live in the southwestern United States. They are also found in parts of Arkansas and Mexico. They mostly live in dry deserts and grasslands.

APPEARANCE

Western diamondback rattlesnakes are grayish brown to reddish brown. Dark diamond shapes cover their bodies. These snakes have triangular heads. Special scales at the end of their tails make up their rattles.

DIET

These rattlesnakes use pit organs to hunt small mammals, reptiles, and birds at night. They strike prey with their fangs to deliver venom.

SPECIES PROFILE

EASTERN DIAMONDBACK RATTLESNAKE

- **Range:** southeastern U.S.
- **Known for:** Eastern diamondbacks are the largest venomous snakes in North America. They can grow up to 8 feet (2.4 meters) long. They weigh up to 10 pounds (4.5 kilograms).

EASTERN COPPERHEADS

Eastern copperheads are venomous but nonaggressive snakes. They are one of five copperhead subspecies.

APPEARANCE

Eastern copperheads have triangular, copper-colored heads. Their bodies are often pinkish tan with a dark hourglass pattern.

DIET

These ambush hunters detect mice and other small animals with heat sensors. They quickly deliver venom with their fangs. They eat the animal after it stops moving.

SIZE COMPARISON

3FT (0.9 m)

1.7FT (0.5 m)

18FT (5.5 m)

eastern copperhead

scarlet kingsnake

king cobra

WHERE DO THEY LIVE?

These copperheads mostly live in the eastern U.S. They prefer woodlands, rocky areas, and swamps.

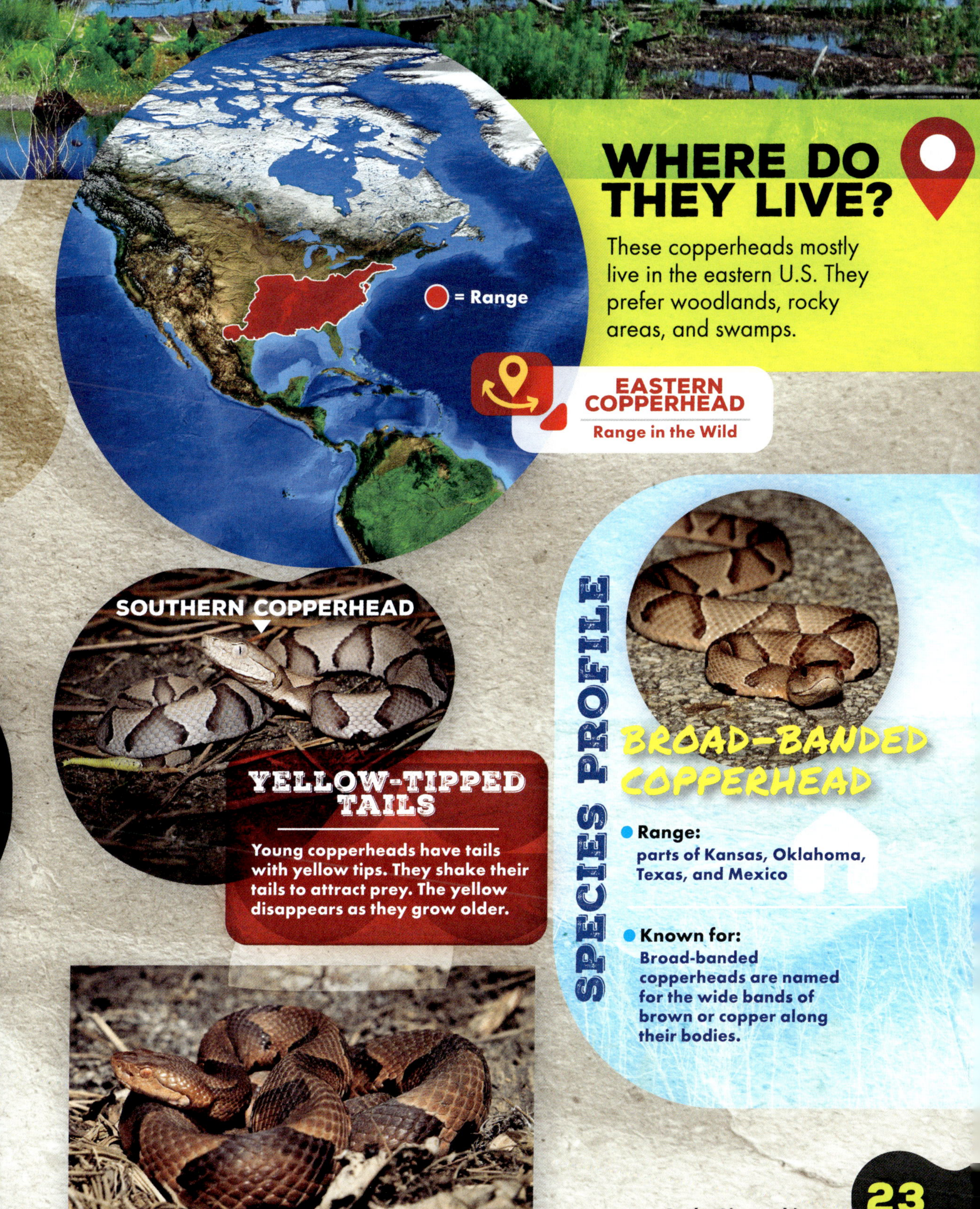

YELLOW-TIPPED TAILS

Young copperheads have tails with yellow tips. They shake their tails to attract prey. The yellow disappears as they grow older.

SPECIES PROFILE

BROAD-BANDED COPPERHEAD

- **Range:** parts of Kansas, Oklahoma, Texas, and Mexico
- **Known for:** Broad-banded copperheads are named for the wide bands of brown or copper along their bodies.

KING COBRAS

King cobras are the longest venomous snakes in the world. They are known for raising their heads and stretching their necks into a hood when threatened.

APPEARANCE

King cobras are brown, black, green, or yellow. White or yellow markings cover their bodies.

NESTS

King cobras are the only snakes that are known to build nests for their eggs.

KING COBRA EGGS

SIZE COMPARISON

2.8FT (0.9 m)

common garter snake

1.7FT (0.5 m)

scarlet kingsnake

18FT (5.5 m)

king cobra

= Range

KING COBRA

Range in the Wild

WHERE DO THEY LIVE?

These cobras live in parts of southern Asia and much of Southeast Asia. They are found near streams in forests and swamps.

SPECIES PROFILE

EGYPTIAN COBRA

- **Range:** northern Africa
- **Known for:** Images of Egyptian cobras were often carved on the crowns of ancient Egyptian rulers. The snakes were symbols of gods and protectors.

DIET

King cobras get their name from hunting other snakes, even other cobras! They mostly hunt during the day. They bite prey with their fangs. Their venom quickly causes the animal's body to shut down.

COMMON GARTER SNAKES

Common garter snakes are one of the most frequently spotted snakes in North America. There are 13 subspecies.

SAN FRANSICO GARTER SNAKE

= Range

WHERE DO THEY LIVE?

These snakes are found throughout most of North America. They live in grassy areas near streams or lakes.

DIET

Common garter snakes use their strong senses of vision and smell to hunt frogs, snails, rodents, birds, and insects. Once they bite prey, their toxic saliva makes the animal still. They swallow food whole.

SIZE COMPARISON

13FT (4 m)
boa constrictor

18FT (5.5 m)
king cobra

2.8FT (0.9 m)
common garter snake

EASTERN GARTER SNAKE

COMMON GARTER SNAKE

APPEARANCE

These snakes are black, gray, olive, or brown. Most have three yellow stripes that run the length of their bodies. Some have scattered red spots. Their skin is bumpy.

SPECIES PROFILE

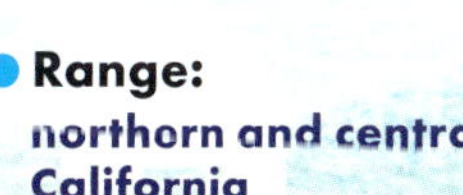

GIANT GARTER SNAKE

- **Range:** northern and central California
- **Known for:** Giant garter snakes are one of the largest and rarest garter snake species. They can grow up to 5.3 feet (1.6 meters) long.

RED-SIDED GARTER SNAKES

SNAKE FRIENDS

Most snakes live alone. But garter snakes are social. They form friend groups that are often led by females.

SCARLET KINGSNAKES

Scarlet kingsnakes are named after their bright red bands.

DIET

These snakes mostly hunt lizards and small snakes at night. They squeeze their prey until it stops breathing.

APPEARANCE

Scarlet kingsnakes have small heads and pointed snouts. They have thin bodies with red, black, and yellow bands.

SIZE COMPARISON

3FT (0.9 m)
North American copperhead

23FT (7 m)

Burmese python

1.7FT (0.5 m)

scarlet kingsnake

WHERE DO THEY LIVE?

Scarlet kingsnakes are found in the southeastern U.S. They live in prairies and wet pinelands. These shy snakes often hide under logs and rocks. Brumation happens underground or in rotting logs and pine trees.

SPECIES PROFILE

EASTERN CORAL SNAKE

- **Range:** southeastern U.S.
- **Known for:** Highly venomous eastern coral snakes have similar red, yellow, and black bands to scarlet kingsnakes. Scarlet kingsnakes may flash their colorful bands so predators think they are eastern coral snakes.

YELLOW-BELLIED SEA SNAKES

Yellow-bellied sea snakes are venomous snakes that live in the sea. They can swim forward and backward.

WHERE DO THEY LIVE?

These snakes live in the warm waters of the Pacific and Indian Oceans. They are commonly seen near the surface in open waters.

SPECIES PROFILE

OLIVE-HEADED SEA SNAKE

- **Range:**
  eastern Indian Ocean and western central Pacific Ocean
- **Known for:**
  These sea snakes are highly venomous. They mostly live in coral reefs.

YELLOW-BELLIED SEA SNAKE
Range in the Wild

● = Range

PADDLE-SHAPED TAIL

SIZE COMPARISON

2.8FT (0.9 m)	18FT (5.5m)	3.6FT (1.1 m)

common garter snake	king cobra	yellow-bellied sea snake

APPEARANCE

Yellow-bellied sea snakes have slender bodies that are black or dark brown. Their bellies are yellow. They have paddle-shaped tails with black markings.

DIET

These sea snakes ambush fish during the day. They often wait at the water's surface for fish to swim close. Then they quickly bite prey with their short fangs to deliver venom. These snakes often hunt in groups.

MANGROVE SNAKES

Mangrove snakes are slightly venomous. They are also called gold-ringed cat snakes. There are currently nine subspecies.

SIZE COMPARISON

3FT (0.9 m)	8FT (2.4 m)	2.8FT (0.9 m)

North American copperhead	mangrove snake	common garter snake

SIMILAR LOOKS

Mangrove snakes look very similar to highly venomous banded kraits.

SPECIES PROFILE

GREEN CAT SNAKE

- **Range:** parts of Southeast Asia and China
- **Known for:** Green cat snakes have green, grayish green, or bluish green backs. Young green cat snakes are reddish brown with green heads.

BANDED KRAIT

APPEARANCE

Mangrove snakes have black bodies with yellow bands. They have yellow scales on their faces. Their vertical pupils help them see well at night.

DIET

These snakes leave tree branches to hunt small reptiles, mammals, and birds on the forest floor at night. Their rear fangs help them bite and keep prey in their mouths.

WHERE DO THEY LIVE?

Mangrove snakes are native to parts of Southeast Asia. These tree-dwelling snakes live in mangroves and forests near rivers.

SIDEWINDERS

Sidewinders are venomous rattlesnakes. These snakes are named for their sideways movements. There are three subspecies.

SIDEWINDER
Range in the Wild

= Range

APPEARANCE

Sidewinders have wide triangular heads with hornlike scales over their eyes. Their brown, gray, or cream bodies match their desert habitats.

WHERE DO THEY LIVE?

These snakes live in the sandy deserts of the southwestern U.S. and northwestern Mexico. Brumation happens in burrows in winter.

SIZE COMPARISON

2.8FT (0.9 m)

common garter snake

18FT (5.5m)

king cobra

2FT (0.6 m)

sidewinder

DIET

Sidewinders bury their bodies in sand to ambush reptiles and rodents. Their heat sensors and sense of smell detect prey nearby. Then they strike with their fangs to deliver deadly venom.

SPECIES PROFILE

MOJAVE DESERT SIDEWINDER

- **Range:** Mojave Desert, U.S.

- **Known for:** These snakes tend to spend time near desert areas with dense vegetation where mammal burrows are found.

S MOVEMENT!

Sidewinders' unusual movement makes them the fastest of all rattlesnakes. Their top speed is 18 miles (29 kilometers) per hour.

BLACK MAMBAS

Black mambas are often called the deadliest snakes in the world. They are named after the black color of their mouths. They show their mouths when threatened. Black mambas are one of four mamba species.

DIET

These snakes use their excellent vision and sense of smell to find small mammals. They quickly attack prey with one or two venomous bites. They follow prey until it stops moving.

= Range

WHERE DO THEY LIVE?

Black mambas are native to southern and eastern Africa. They are found in savannas, woodlands, and rocky areas.

SIZE COMPARISON

5FT (1.5 m)	14FT (4.3m)	1.7FT (0.5 m)
western diamondback rattlesnake	black mamba	scarlet kingsnake

APPEARANCE

Black mambas have long, slender bodies that are olive, brown, or gray. They flatten their necks to create a hood when they are threatened.

THE FASTEST!

Black mambas are among the fastest snakes in the world. They can travel up to 12.5 miles (20 kilometers) per hour.

SPECIES PROFILE

EASTERN GREEN MAMBA

- **Range:** southern East Africa
- **Known for:** Unlike some mamba species, these snakes stay hidden in trees. They typically do not attack humans.

CORN SNAKES

Corn snakes are nonvenomous constrictors that are often kept as pets. Their name may come from belly markings that look like corn kernels. They are sometimes called red rat snakes.

APPEARANCE

These thin snakes have orange or brown bodies with reddish-brown patches outlined in black. A black-and-white checkered pattern covers their bellies.

DIET

These hunters prey on rodents and birds. They also eat eggs. They bite their prey before tightly wrapping their bodies around it.

SIZE COMPARISON

3FT (0.9 m)

North American copperhead

18FT (5.5 m)

king cobra

6FT (1.8 m)

corn snake

WHERE DO THEY LIVE?

Corn snakes are found in the eastern and southeastern U.S. They have been introduced to several islands in the Caribbean. They prefer meadows, woodlands, and rocky areas.

= Range

A LONG LIFE

Corn snakes can live more than 20 years as pets. The oldest corn snake lived for 32 years.

SPECIES PROFILE

GREAT PLAINS RAT SNAKE

- **Range:** central U.S. and northern Mexico
- **Known for:** These nonvenomous snakes will bite when threatened or bothered. They may rattle their tails to make threats think they are rattlesnakes.

NORTHERN WATER SNAKES

Northern water snakes are harmless. But they are often mistaken as venomous water moccasins.

WHERE DO THEY LIVE?

These snakes live in eastern and central North America. They are found in and near freshwater lakes and riverbanks. They also spend time in shrubs.

DIET

These snakes swim through schools of fish with their mouths open, scooping fish up. They also grab fish and frogs with their long bodies.

SIZE COMPARISON

3.5FT (1.1 m)

northern water snake

8FT (2.4 m)

mangrove snake

2.8FT (0.9 m)

common garter snake

APPEARANCE

These thick snakes have wide brown, black, or reddish crossbands. Narrow bands of gray or tan also mark their bodies. Rough, raised scales cover their backs.

SMELLY WHEN SCARED

These snakes give off a bad-smelling odor mixed with waste whenever they feel threatened.

SPECIES PROFILE

CARIBBEAN WATER SNAKE

- **Range:** Cuba, Cayman Islands
- **Known for:** These snakes prefer fresh water, but they can handle salt water for short periods.

SNAKES AND
PEOPLE

Snakes have long been popular in many cultures. In Irish and Norse mythology, snakes are often shown as dangerous monsters. Chinese and Egyptian myths describe them as powerful and wise. The ancient Greeks believed that snakes had a healing power.

ANCIENT EGYPTIAN ART

HYGIEIA, GREEK GODDESS OF HEALTH

THE JUNGLE BOOK

SNAKES AND MEDICINE

Snake venom is used today to make medicine for many health conditions.

▲ COLLECTING SNAKE VENOM

Despite having influence throughout history, snakes face many threats today. Fear drives many human behaviors that harm snakes. Some are hunted for their skin or their meat. The pet trade often takes wild snakes out of their natural habitats. It also leads to some species becoming invasive. This disrupts food chains, harming habitats and animals.

FOLKLORE PROFILE

NAME:

MEDUSA

COUNTRY:

GREECE

FAMOUS FOR:

In Greek mythology, Medusa was a winged female creature with a head full of snakes for hair. Anyone who looked at her would instantly turn to stone.

Many snake species face habitat loss from climate change and deforestation. This forces them to adapt and change their behaviors. Many move to new areas, often closer to humans.

Many organizations are working to protect snakes. They help pass laws that keep snakes and their habitats safe. They work to restore and rebuild damaged habitats. Other laws prevent certain snake species from being captured as pets. Organizations also teach people how to live peacefully with snakes and not fear them. Learning about snakes and working together can help these animals survive.

GLOSSARY

adapted—changed over a period of time

aggressive—ready to fight

ambush—to attack from a hiding place

bask—to lie in the sun; cold-blooded animals often bask to raise their body temperatures.

brumation—sluggish behavior or inactivity that reptiles show in cold weather

burrows—tunnels or holes in the ground that some animals use for homes

climate change—long-term changes to Earth's weather and climate

coil—to form a series of loops

constriction—the act of squeezing

cultures—societies that hold the same beliefs, arts, and ways of life

deforestation—the act of cutting down a wide area of trees

diverse—made up of animals that are different from one another

evolve—to change from one form into a new form

flexible—able to bend easily

habitats—natural homes of plants and animals

invasive—an organism that is not native to the place it is found and likely to take over native species and ecosystems

mammals—warm-blooded animals that have backbones and feed their young milk

mangroves—trees and shrubs in coastal areas that grow densely together

mythology—a collection of stories and ideas from a certain group or culture

native—belonging to a specific place by birth

parasites—living things that use other living things to survive; parasites harm their hosts.

pheromones—chemicals produced by animals that serve to attract individuals of the same species

pit organs—body parts that help some snakes sense heat

rainforests—tropical woodlands that receive heavy rainfall

saliva—a watery fluid in the mouth

savannas—grasslands with scattered trees

species—groups of living things that are alike and can reproduce with one another; subspecies are particular types of animals that exist within a species.

stalk—to hunt slowly and quietly

venom—a poisonous substance made by some animals, including snakes

WRITE ABOUT IT!

- What species of snake would you like to learn more about? **Why?**
- Do you have a favorite snake species? **What** is it and **why?**
- **What** changes can you make in your life that could help keep snakes safe?

INDEX

The images in this book are reproduced through the courtesy of: Miroslav Srb, front cover (Boa), p. 19 (top right); asbtkb, front cover (rattlesnake), pp. 12 (western diamondback rattlesnake), 19 (bottom), 21 (top right); DS light photography, cover (cobra); NickEvansKZN, front cover (black mamba), p. 31 (paddle-shaped tail); Eric Isselée, front cover (corn snake), pp. 8 (corn snake hatching), 20-21 (appearance), 24 (appearance); Gabriele Maltinti, front cover (vegetation); olegkruglyak3, pp. 2-3 (blue sky), 6 (blue sky), 10-11 (blue sky), 42-43 (blue sky); Glebstock, pp. 2-3 (Philippines), 9 (Philippines), 12-13 (Philippines); Narupon, p. 3 (pit viper); muhammadAwais, p. 3 (bottom snake); mgkuijpers, pp. 4-5 (top), 5 (great lakes bush viper), 26 (San Fransico garter snake), 33 (pupil), 36 (middle); Mark Kostich, pp. 4 (bush viper, shedding scales), 9 (bush viper snakelet), 11 (amazon tree boa molting), 12 (sidewinders); Richard Carey, p. 5 (banded sea snake); JUAN CARLOS MUNOZ, p. 6 (snake fossil); Adisha, p. 6 (olive sea snake); Sean, p. 6 (emerald tree boa); brm1949, p. 6 (flexible jaw); Maizal, p. 7 (top); stuporter, p. 7 (jaw); Joe McDonald, p. 7 (teeth); Olga, p. 8 (snake egg); Breck P. Kent, p. 8 (garter snake); Tom, pp. 9 (western diamondback rattlesnake), 20 (top); hin255, p. 9 (green anaconda); Ken Griffiths, pp. 9 (yellow-bellied sea snake), 13 (yellow-bellied sea snakes), 30-31 (appearance), 31 (bottom left); Volodymyr Shevchuk, p. 9 (king cobra); DEVJYOTI, p. 10 (top); Gregory, pp. 10 (middle), 21 (pit organ); Nicholas J. Klein, p. 10 (bottom); Gabriela Bertolini, p. 11 (snake skin); Jiri Prochazka, p. 11 (brown forest cobra); Morrow Newbury, p. 12 (Burmese python); Luis, p. 12 (green anacondas); Karlos Lomsky, pp. 12 (Boa constrictors), 19 (diet); Amol, p. 12 (north American copperheads); Tomasz, p. 12 (king cobras); Craig, p. 13 (black mambas); Natalia Kuzmina, p. 13 (common garter snakes); ondreicka, p. 13 (scarlet kingsnakes); dwi, pp. 13 (mangrove snakes), 14 (top), 32 (bottom); Hamilton, pp. 13 (corn snakes), 39 (left middle), 40 (top); saiko3p, p. 14 (Thailand); kuritafsheen, pp. 14 (bottom), 24 (top); Heiko Kiera, pp. 15 (top, middle right); Ade, p. 15 (appearance); Lunatic_67/ Getty Images, p. 15 (bottom); vaclav, pp. 16-17 (Venezuela); ShutterOK, p. 16 (top); Nynke, pp. 16-17 (appearance), 38 (appearance); gudkovandrey, p. 16 (middle); slowmotiongli, pp. 16 (bottom), 32 (green cat snake); Fernando Flores/ Wikimedia, p. 17 (top); Francois Gohier/ Science Source, p. 17 (middle); FotoRequest, p. 17 (bottom); christian vinces, pp. 18-19 (Amazon jungle); bennytrapp, pp. 18 (top), 18-19 (appearance), 22 (appearance); franciscoalberto, p. 18; Honza Hejda, p. 19 (top left); Jason Yoder, pp. 20-21 (Sonoran Desert); markskalny, p. 20 (middle); Lauren, pp. 21 (rattle), 45 (bottom right); Chase D'Animulls, pp. 21 (eastern Diamondback rattlesnake), 28-29 (Florida); neon444, p. 22 (Great Dismal swamp); Jay Ondreicka, pp. 22 (top), 41 (left bottom); RMMPPhotography, p. 22 (bottom); Clint H, p. 23 (southern copperhead); David McGowen, p. 23 (broad-banded copperhead); Mike Wilhelm, pp. 23 (bottom), 27 (eastern Garter snake), 28 (top); boyloso, pp. 24-25 (Thailand); Panupong, p. 24 (king cobra eggs); alinamd, p. 25 (top); Ghorayr/ Wikimedia, p. 25 (Egyptian cobra); Padodo, p. 25 (diet); Lost_in_ the_Midwest, pp. 26-27 (South Dakota); Ivan Kuzmin, p. 26 (middle); Gerry, p. 26 (bottom); Michael, p. 27 (common garter snake); Dave Feliz (Yolodave)/ Wikimedia, p. 27 (giant garter snake); Mark Lotterhand, p. 27 (red-sided garter snakes); Stan, p. 28 (appearance); Radiant Reptilia, p. 29 (top, bottom); daniel_e/ iNaturalist/ Wikimedia, p. 29 (eastern coral snake); imageBROKER. com/ Alamy Stock Photo, p. 29 (middle); Fyle, pp. 30-31 (Ngapali Beach); John Fader, p. 30 (top left); Claire Goiran/ Wikimedia, p. 30 (olive-headed sea snake); Auscape/ Contributor/ Getty Images, p. 31 (bottom right); anemone, pp. 32-33 (Indonesia); lessysebastian, p. 32 (top); RealityImages, p. 32 (Branded Krait); fivespots, pp. 33 (appearance), 34 (bottom); zinkevych, p. 33 (diet); Alisa, pp. 34-35 (Mojave desert); Frost, p. 34 (top); Victorrocha/ Wikimedia, p. 35; Wildspaces, p. 35 (Mojave desert sidewinder); MSMondadori, p. 35 (middle); Fine Art Photos, p. 35 (bottom); dougholder, pp. 36-37 (South Africa); reptiles4all, p. 36 (top); Nick Greaves, p. 36 (bottom); Craig Cordier, p. 37 (top, appearance, bottom); Henner Damke, p. 37 (eastern green mamba); Felix Mizioznikov, pp. 38-39 (South Africa); MichaelL, p. 38 (top); alan1951, p. 38 (bottom); Matt Jeppson, p. 39 (great plains rat snake); Dennis W Donohue, p. 39 (bottom); Fotoluminate LLC, pp. 40-41 (Florida Nature Preserve); Michiel de Wit, pp. 40-41 (appearance); Colin Temple, p. 40 (bottom); Katie Flenker, p. 41 (top); Brian Lasenby, p. 41 (right bottom); CK-TravelPhotos, p. 42 (ancient Egyptian art); alt Disney Studios Motion Pictures/ courtesy Everett Collection, p. 42 (The Jungle Book); Print Collector/ Contributor/ Getty Images, p. 42 (Hygieia, Greek goddess of health); EM DAROUTH, p. 42 (bottom); Yongkiet Jitwattanatam, p. 43 (collecting snake venom); Debra Heaphy/ Wikimedia, p. 43 (medusa); nobuyuki miyaho, p. 44 (top); MichaelSvoboda/ Getty Images, p. 44 (snake wrangler); Audrey Snider-Bell, p. 44 (left bottom); poco_bw/ Getty Images, p. 44 (right bottom); Pacific Press/ Contributor/ Getty Images, p. 45 (top); Kev Gregory, p. 45 (bottom left).